McCall

by Iain Gray

WRITING *to* REMEMBER

WRITING *to* REMEMBER

79 Main Street, Newtongrange,
Midlothian EH22 4NA
Tel: 0131 344 0414   Fax: 0845 075 6085
E-mail: info@lang-syne.co.uk
www.langsyneshop.co.uk

Design by Dorothy Meikle
Printed by Printwell Ltd
© Lang Syne Publishers Ltd 2021

All rights reserved. No part of this publication may be reproduced, stored or introduced into a retrieval system, or transmitted in any form or by any means (electronic, mechanical, photocopying, recording or otherwise) without the prior written permission of Lang Syne Publishers Ltd.

ISBN 978-1-85217-765-2

McCall

MOTTO:
By sea and by land
(MacDonald)

CREST:
A hand in armour holding a cross-crosslet

TERRITORIES include:
Islay, Sleat on Isle of Skye, Kintyre

NAME variations include:
Macall
Mccall
Mccoll
MacColl
MacCole
MacCall
MacAul

Chapter one:

The origins of the clan system

by Rennie McOwan

The original Scottish clans of the Highlands and the great families of the Lowlands and Borders were gatherings of families, relatives, allies and neighbours for mutual protection against rivals or invaders.

Scotland experienced invasion from the Vikings, the Romans and English armies from the south. The Norman invasion of what is now England also had an influence on land-holding in Scotland. Some of these invaders stayed on and in time became 'Scottish'.

The word clan derives from the Gaelic language term 'clann', meaning children, and it was first used many centuries ago as communities were formed around tribal lands in glens and mountain fastnesses.

The format of clans changed over the centuries, but at its best the chief and his family held the land on behalf of all, like trustees, and the ordinary clansmen and women believed they had a blood relationship with the founder of their clan.

There were two way duties and obligations. An inadequate chief could be deposed and replaced by someone of greater ability.

Clan people had an immense pride in race. Their relationship with the chief was like adult children to a father and they had a real dignity.

The concept of clanship is very old and a more feudal notion of authority gradually crept in.

Pictland, for instance, was divided into seven principalities ruled by feudal leaders who were the strongest and most charismatic leaders of their particular groups.

By the sixth century the 'British' kingdoms of Strathclyde, Lothian and Celtic Dalriada (Argyll) had emerged and Scotland, as one nation, began to take shape in the time of King Kenneth MacAlpin.

Some chiefs claimed descent from ancient kings which may not have been accurate in every case.

By the twelfth and thirteenth centuries the clans and families were more strongly brought under the central control of Scottish monarchs.

Lands were awarded and administered more and more under royal favour, yet the power of the area clan chiefs was still very great.

The long wars to ensure Scotland's

independence against the expansionist ideas of English monarchs extended the influence of some clans and reduced the lands of others.

Those who supported Scotland's greatest king, Robert the Bruce, were awarded the territories of the families who had opposed his claim to the Scottish throne.

In the Scottish Borders country – the notorious Debatable Lands – the great families built up a ferocious reputation for providing warlike men accustomed to raiding into England and occasionally fighting one another.

Chiefs had the power to dispense justice and to confiscate lands and clan warfare produced a society where martial virtues – courage, hardiness, tenacity – were greatly admired.

Gradually the relationship between the clans and the Crown became strained as Scottish monarchs became more orientated to life in the Lowlands and, on occasion, towards England.

The Highland clans spoke a different language, Gaelic, whereas the language of Lowland Scotland and the court was Scots and in more modern times, English.

Highlanders dressed differently, had different

customs, and their wild mountain land sometimes seemed almost foreign to people living in the Lowlands.

It must be emphasised that Gaelic culture was very rich and story-telling, poetry, piping, the clarsach (harp) and other music all flourished and were greatly respected.

Highland culture was different from other parts of Scotland but it was not inferior or less sophisticated.

Central Government, whether in London or Edinburgh, sometimes saw the Gaelic clans as a challenge to their authority and some sent expeditions into the Highlands and west to crush the power of the Lords of the Isles.

Nevertheless, when the eighteenth century Jacobite Risings came along the cause of the Stuarts was mainly supported by Highland clans.

The word Jacobite comes from the Latin for James – Jacobus. The Jacobites wanted to restore the exiled Stuarts to the throne of Britain.

The monarchies of Scotland and England became one in 1603 when King James VI of Scotland (1st of England) gained the English throne after Queen Elizabeth died.

The Union of Parliaments of Scotland and England, the Treaty of Union, took place in 1707.

Some Highland clans, of course, and Lowland families opposed the Jacobites and supported the incoming Hanoverians.

After the Jacobite cause finally went down at Culloden in 1746 a kind of ethnic cleansing took place. The power of the chiefs was curtailed. Tartan and the pipes were banned in law.

Many emigrated, some because they wanted to, some because they were evicted by force. In addition, many Highlanders left for the cities of the south to seek work.

Many of the clan lands became home to sheep and deer shooting estates.

But the warlike traditions of the clans and the great Lowland and Border families lived on, with their descendants fighting bravely for freedom in two world wars.

Remember the men from whence you came, says the Gaelic proverb, and to that could be added the role of many heroic women.

The spirit of the clan, of having roots, whether Highland or Lowland, means much to thousands of people.

Meanwhile, many families proudly boast the heraldic device known as a Coat of Arms, as featured on our front cover.

The central motif of the Coat of Arms would originally have been what was sometimes borne on the shield of a warrior to distinguish himself from others on the battlefield.

Not featured on the Coat of Arms, but highlighted on page three, is the family motto and related crest – with the latter frequently different from the central motif.

Clan warfare produced a society where courage and tenacity were greatly admired

Chapter two:

Lords of the Isles

A form of 'MacCall' and 'MacColl', the McCall name derives from the Gaelic personal name Coll, or Colla, and denotes 'son of the battle chief.'

This martial derivation is apt, with the McCalls, predominantly known in earliest times in the Scottish Highlands and Islands as 'MacColl', embroiled for centuries in bitter and bloody internecine clan warfare.

Untangling what is a complex genealogy, it can be determined that they can ultimately be traced back to the mighty Clan Donald, or Clan MacDonald, one of the oldest and largest clans and boasting a host of septs, or sub-branches.

Derived from the Gaelic *clanna*, meaning 'children', a clan was a close-knit tribal grouping settled in a particular territory and whose members – or 'children', or 'kin' – owed unswerving loyalty to a chief who, in turn, was bound by duty and honour to protect them.

Not all members of a clan, such as the McCalls/MacColls, necessarily shared the same surname as the chief – known as *ceann-cinnidh*, meaning 'head and chief of the family' – and these 'kindred of the clan', or 'kinsfolk', were recognised, as they are to this day, as septs of the clan.

As such, they are entitled to share in the clan's heritage and traditions that include the right to display its tartan and heraldry of crest and motto – this heraldry recognised by the Lord Lyon King of Arms of Scotland, the final arbiter on all matters heraldic.

In the case of the McCalls/MacColls, they share the Clan Donald motto 'By sea and by land' and crest of an arm in armour holding a cross-crosslet.

Branches of Clan Donald are Clan Macdonald of Clanranald, Clan MacDonell of Glengarry, Clan Macdonald of Sleat, Clan MacDonald of Keppoch and Clan MacAlister.

All these clans have recognised chiefs, while those without are Clan MacDonald of Lochalsh, Clan MacDonald of Dunnyveg, the MacDonalds of Glencoe and the MacDonalds of Ardnamurchan – while the MacDonnells of Antrim are a cadet branch of the MacDonalds of Dunnyveg.

The McCalls/MacColls, in addition to overall being recognised as a sept of Clan Donald, are septs of both the Macdonalds of Sleat and the MacDonalds of Dunnyveg – and their early history is in effect the history of these two latter clans in particular and Clan Donald in general.

With a majestic pedigree, Clan Donald traces a descent from Dòmhnall Mac Raghnaill, who died in about 1250 and whose father Ranald was King of the Isles and Lord of Argyll and Kintyre.

Ranald, in turn, was a son of one of the most colourful and charismatic figures to grace the pages of the drama that is Scotland's early history.

This was Somerled, and it is through their proud descent from him that a rich and heady brew of both Norse and Celtic blood courses through the veins of the MacDonalds and their kinsfolk such as the McCalls/MacColls to this day.

By the mid-twelfth century, Somerled, or Somhairle, whose name means 'summer wanderer' or 'summer sailor', had carved out a vast west coast fiefdom that included the south isles from Bute to Ardnamurchan Point in addition to Kintyre, Argyll and Lorne.

Fiercely independent, he considered he owed allegiance to no man, not least the King of Scots.

It was following the death of King David I in

1153 that his grandson, Malcolm, succeeded to the throne as King Malcolm IV.

He inherited a troubled kingdom torn apart by not only civil warfare on the mainland but the threat of invasion from the north by Vikings, who sacked Aberdeen in the same year that he succeeded to the throne, and invasion from the west in the form of Somerled.

A powerful group of ambitious magnates, mainly centred in the Moray area in the northeast of Scotland, resolved to depose Malcolm, replacing him with their own puppet king, and were joined in this bold venture by Somerled, who was always eager to exploit any opportunity for warfare and plunder.

In 1157, one year after he defeated his wife's brother Godfred, the King of Man, in a sea battle off Islay, in the Inner Hebrides, Somerled seized control of the islands of Bute and Arran.

Possession of these strategically important islands increased the threat he posed to the west coast mainland and Malcolm, rather naively, sought to resolve the problem by ordering Somerled to surrender his domains into the hands of the Crown, thereafter holding them as a mere vassal.

Somerled's answer was predictable.

He assembled a 15,000 strong force of kinsmen and, embarking in a fleet of 164 swift galleys, sailed up the Firth of Clyde and then up the River Clyde to sack the town of Glasgow in a blood-crazed orgy of arson, rape and plunder.

Malcolm's loyal magnate in the west, Walter Fitzalan, the High Steward, hastily assembled a rag-tag force of other loyal magnates and their retainers.

Somerled, eager to face the challenge, met the woefully inadequate royal army at Renfrew.

Accounts differ on what now actually transpired on that bitterly cold day of January 1, 1164.

One account is that a fierce battle ensued and, as Somerled's battle-hardened Islesmen rapidly gained the upper hand over the royal forces, the tide of battle turned when Somerled received a mortal thrust from a spear.

Dismayed at the loss of their leader, the Islesmen's discipline broke down, and hundreds were slaughtered as they fled back to their galleys.

Walter Fitzalan had, against all the odds, achieved not only victory over a much superior force, but crushed the threat to the throne.

A rather less heroic account of the victory, however, is that the High Steward had realised he had no realistic hope of defeating Somerled in a set-piece battle and, accordingly, bribed Maurice MacNeill, Somerled's nephew, to murder his uncle.

MacNeill accomplished this treacherous deed by gaining admittance to Somerled's tent after his army had encamped at Renfrew and stabbing him through the heart, possibly while he slept.

Somerled's domains subsequently split up among his sons, and through this he is recognised as the progenitor or founder of the mighty MacDonald Lords of the Isles.

By 1493, inter-clan feuding in the Highlands and Islands had reached such a stage of anarchy, with royal authority being flouted at every turn, that King James IV finally annexed the Lordship of the Isles to the Crown, with the monarch himself assuming the title of Lord of the Isles.

Today the Court of the Lord Lyon recognises the title of 'High Chief of Clan Donald' while the 'spiritual home' of the clan is the magnificent Armadale Castle and Gardens at Sleat, on the Isle of Skye.

Once the seat of the Macdonalds of Sleat, it is now home to the Museum of the Isles and the Clan Donald Centre.

Chapter three:

Innovation and enterprise

In later centuries and in more peaceful endeavours and pursuits, Dr Annie McCall was a pioneer in the field of midwifery.

Born in Manchester in 1859, it was after studying on the continent and then at the London School of Medicine for Women, that in 1885 she became one of the first women to qualify as a doctor.

At a time when midwifery techniques were rather primitive, four years after qualifying and along with Miss Marion Ritchie, she opened the Clapham Maternity Hospital, London, staffed entirely by women doctors and students.

Offering both antenatal and postnatal care and setting high standards in hygiene along with advice on nutrition and exercise, the hospital, renamed the Annie McCall Maternity Hospital in 1936, achieved very low death rates among patients.

These rates were particularly high in poorer

areas because of a combination of factors that included not only social deprivation, but also resultant unhealthy lifestyles while, as a member of the Temperance Society, Dr McCall did not allow patients or her nurses to drink alcohol.

The hospital had to close after being bombed during the Second World War blitz on London, but was rebuilt following Dr McCall's death in 1949; converted to residential use in 2014, the building now has Grade II listed status.

In the field of animal welfare, James McCall was the Scottish veterinary surgeon who was the founder and first principal of Glasgow Veterinary College.

Born in 1834 in Newton on Ayr, South Ayrshire, one of his first jobs was a superintendent of the horse department of the Pickford haulage company, before studying at the Royal (Dick) Veterinary College, Edinburgh.

Practising for a time as a vet in the village of Symington, East Ayrshire, he later became professor of anatomy and physiology at his old alma-mater in Edinburgh before moving to Glasgow to begin teaching a few students.

As the number of students grew, he applied

for a royal charter to open a veterinary college and this was granted in 1863 – allowing students of the new Glasgow Veterinary College to study and take examinations to qualify for membership of the Royal College of Veterinary Surgeons.

Also president of the Clydesdale Horse Society, he died in 1915.

Displaying skill not only on the football pitch but also a flair for commercial enterprise, Robert Smyth McColl was the Scottish centre forward who, along with his brother, laid the foundations for the news, convenience and variety stores RS McColl.

Born in Glasgow in 1876, he started playing for local amateur club Queen's Park in 1894.

A spell south of the border followed, playing as a professional for Newcastle United, and then returning to his home city in 1904 to play for Rangers.

Returning as an amateur to his old club Queen's Park, towards the end of his playing career in 1912 he scored six goals against Port Glasgow Athletic – a Scottish scoring record.

Having also scored 13 goals for the Scottish national team, he died in 1959 and was inducted into the Scottish Football Hall of Fame in 2011.

Meanwhile, having served throughout the

First World War as a sergeant in the Royal Army Service Corps and with his footballing career at an end, he focussed his full attention on a sweet shop business he had opened along with his brother Tom in 1901.

Located in Albert Drive, in Glasgow's Pollokshields district and known simply as R.S. McColl – the 'R' and 'S' the initials of his forename and middle name, respectively – their first shop proved popular and the business rapidly expanded, with Robert McColl nicknamed "Toffee Bob" because of his confectionery.

A factory was opened in North Woodside Road to cope with growing demand, while the business expanded to more than 30 branches throughout Scotland.

Restructuring the enterprise as a limited company in 1925 and, eight years later, selling his controlling interest to the Cadbury group, the McColl brothers remained as salaried employees.

Diversifying into the sale of other products including newspapers and tobacco, branches were opened throughout England and by 1935 there were 180 branches, employing more than 800 people, throughout the UK.

The brothers retired in 1946 and the business has subsequently experienced a number of changes in ownership.

Becoming part of TM Retail in 1998 and renamed Martin McColl Limited in 2006 having acquired the Martin Retail Group, some stores were re-branded 'Martins' or 'McColls'.

But not in Scotland, where the proud name RS McColl is retained in honour of its enterprising, footballing founder.

On American shores and in a mystery that remains unsolved to this day, Stacy McCall was one of three women who inexplicably disappeared from a friend's home in Springfield, Missouri, on June 7, 1992.

Known as 'The Springfield Three', numerous efforts to trace them have failed, with investigators having pursued a number of leads that have frustratingly led nowhere.

Aged 18 at the time of her disappearance, the last known positive whereabouts of Stacy had been at the home of her friend Suzie Streeter, aged 19 and Suzie's unmarried mother 47-year-old Sherrill Levitt.

The two teenagers had attended a graduation party on the evening of their disappearance, returning to spend the night at the home Suzie shared with her mother in East Delmar Street.

Friends called on the house the following morning when Stacy and Suzie failed to arrive for a planned meeting and, while all their possessions including purses, clothing and jewellery were there, there was no sign of the pair or Suzie's mother.

By the time police were called and arrived to examine the house, the only sign of a disturbance was a smashed porch light, but the scene had been unwittingly contaminated by friends who arrived before police.

Possible leads included a recorded phone message one of the friends had listened to – but this was accidentally deleted before investigators could listen to it.

With the three women believed to have been abducted, a nationwide investigation was launched and, on December 31, a man called the hotline of the television show *America's Most Wanted* with "prime knowledge of the abductions", police said.

But the call was disconnected as the switchboard operator attempted to link up with investigators in Springfield.

Although the missing women were legally

declared dead in 1997, their case remains open and listed under "missing".

Also in 1997, convicted murderer and robber Robert Craig Cox, imprisoned in Texas, told journalists he knew the women had been murdered and where they were buried, but that their bodies would never be recovered.

Intriguingly, Cox had been living with his parents in Springfield at the time of the disappearances – but police remain unconvinced of the veracity of his claims, while he has stated he will not divulge more until after his mother is dead.

The mysterious case of 'The Springfield Three' has meanwhile been the subject of a number of theories and newspaper and magazine articles in addition to television shows including *Investigation Discovery* and *48 Hours*.

Also on American shores, and in an earlier century, John 'Jack' McCall was the drifter who has the dubious distinction of being the murderer of Wild West legend Wild Bill Hickok.

Born in about 1852 in Jefferson County, Kentucky and also known as 'Broken Nose Jack' or 'Crooked Nose', he had drifted west from his home state to become a buffalo hunter and by 1876, under the alias 'Bill Sutherland', was living in a gold mining camp outside Deadwood, in Dakota Territory.

On August 1, 1876, he had been drinking in Nuttal and Mann's saloon in Deadwood, while Wild Bill was playing in a card game.

One of the players dropped out and McCall, drunk by this time, joined the game to make up the numbers but quickly lost a lot of hands and ended up broke.

Hickok gave him the friendly advice not to play again until he could cover his losses, and even offered him money to buy his breakfast.

McCall accepted the money, but nevertheless felt insulted and returned to the bar the following evening while Hickok was engaged in another game and, contrary to his normal careful habit, sitting with his back to the door.

McCall pulled out a revolver and, crying out "Damn you! Take that!" shot him through the back of the head, killing him instantly.

Eventually brought to justice, McCall was hanged in March of the following year in Yankton, Dakota Territory.

Back on Scottish shores, one particularly inventive bearer of the McCall name was the Scottish cartwright Thomas McCall who, in 1869, built two versions of the two-wheeled bicycle contraption known as a velocipede.

Born in 1834 in Penpont, Dumfriesshire but moving to Kilmarnock when aged 20, his contraption utilised levers and rods that 'tossed' a crank on the rear wheel to initiate motion – as opposed to French versions that featured front-wheel pedal cranks.

Controversy exists to this day as to whether or not McCall or fellow Dumfriesshire-born inventor Kirkpatrick Fleming should be credited with having invented the 'first true bicycle.'

McCall died in 1904, while a replica of his velocipede – whether or not the 'first true bicycle', but interesting nonetheless – is held in the Dumfries Observatory and Museum.

Chapter four:

On the world stage

In the genre of American 'outlaw' country music, William Dale Fries Jr. is the singer and songwriter better known as C.W. McCall.

Born in 1928 in Audubon, Iowa, he is best known for his 1976 hit *Convoy,* featured in the 1978 film of the name starring Kris Kristofferson, Burt Young, Ali McGraw and Ernest Borgnine.

Awarded a gold disc, the theme of the song and film was the then craze for CB (Citizens' Band) radio particularly favoured by truckers across the United States, and was ranked at No. 98 by *Rolling Stone* magazine in 2014 in its list of 100 Greatest Country Songs.

An inductee of the Iowa Rock 'n' Roll Hall of Fame, McCall's other hits include W*olf Creek Pass*, *Black Bear Road* and *Keep on a-Truckin' Café*.

A co-founder of the American funk/r&b band Con Funk Shun, **Louis McCall Sr.** was the singer, songwriter and drummer born in 1935 in Vallejo, California.

Top hits enjoyed by the band include the

1979 *Chase Me* and, from 1983, *Baby I'm Hooked (Right into Your Love)*, while the seven-piece outfit was honoured by the National R&B Society with a Lifetime Achievement Award in 2014.

This was seven years after McCall was found murdered outside a friend's home in Stone Mountain, Georgia, the apparent victim of a robbery.

With the popular spelling variant 'MacColl', **Ewan MacColl** was the British folk singer, songwriter, actor and labour activist born to Scottish parents in 1915 in Salford, Lancashire.

Born James Henry Miller – and changing it to Ewan MacColl after being inspired by the Scottish language known as Lallans – he became famous for not only his political activisim, expressed through his co-founding in 1946 of the touring Theatre Workshop, but for a vast output of ballads, many written in collaboration with Irish singer and songwriter Dominic Behan.

Married to the theatre director Joan Littlewood, the dancer Jean Newlove and then the American folk singer and activist Peggy Seeger, one of his most famous songs is *The First Time Ever I Saw Your Face*.

Written for Seeger to sing in a play in which she was performing, it became a major international hit when recorded by Roberta Flack in 1972, winning a Grammy Award for Song of the Year.

Inspired by his childhood home of Salford, another hit, *Dirty Old Town*, has been recorded by a number of artists ranging from in 1964 The Spinners, in 1968 Roger Whittaker, in 1970 The Clancy Brothers and, in 2003, Simple Minds.

He died in 1989, while through his second marriage to Jean Newlove he was the father of the singer and songwriter **Kirsty MacColl**.

Born in 1959 in Croydon, London, and with hits throughout the 1980s and 1990s including *There's a Guy Works Down the Chip Shop Swears He's Elvis* and, with the Pogues, *Fairytale of New York*, she was killed in 2000 when struck by a powerboat while diving with her sons in part of the National Marine Park of Cozumel, Mexico.

With his surname an Anglicisation of the Irish Gaelic *Mac Cathmhaoil*, **Patrick McCall** was the songwriter and poet born in Dublin in 1861.

The author of lyrics to traditional Irish airs concerning the Wexford Ballads, a contributor to the Dublin Historical Record and one of the founding members of Ireland's National Literary Society, he died in 1919.

Chosen by the *Guinness Book of Recorded Sound* as 'one of the top ten singers on disc of all time', Peter Smith Dawson was the Australian bass-baritone, born in Adelaide in 1882 to Scottish parents, better known as **P.J. McCall**.

This was one of a number of aliases he employed throughout an international career performing and recording arias, oratorio solos and ballads.

Famed for oratorios including Haydn's *The Creation*, Mendelssohn's *Elijah* and Handel's *Messiah*, he died in 1961.

From music to the highly competitive world of sport, **Andy McCall** was the Scottish footballer born in 1925 in Hamilton, South Lanarkshire; having played as a winger for teams including West Bromwich Albion, Halifax Town and, most notably, Leeds United, he died in 2014.

He was the father of the former midfield player and coach **Stuart McCall**, born in Leeds in 1964.

In addition to earning 40 caps playing for Scotland, he played for teams including Bradford City, Everton, Rangers and Sheffield, and has also managed Rangers and Motherwell.

Also on the football pitch, **Ian McCall** is the Scottish former midfielder who played for teams including Queen's Park, Dunfermline Athletic and Partick Thistle; born in Dumfries in 1964, he has also managed clubs including Falkirk, Dundee United, Queen of the South and Partick Thistle.

From the football pitch to the boxing ring, **Oliver McCall**, born in Chicago in 1965, is the American former boxer who took the world heavyweight title in 1994 after beating British boxer Lennox Lewis; he is the father of the heavyweight boxer **Elijah McCall**, born in Chicago in 1988.

On the ice rink, **Rob McCall** was the Canadian ice dancer who, along with partner Tracy Wilson, was the 1988 Olympic bronze medallist; born in 1958 in Halifax, Nova Scotia, he died in 1991.

From sport to the creative world of the written word, **Alexander McCall Smith** is the highly prolific and best-selling British-Zimbabwean novelist and distinguished expert on medical law and bioethics born in 1948 in Bulawayo, in what was then Southern Rhodesia.

Rather unusually, 'McCall' is not his middle name, his two-part surname being 'McCall Smith' – and not hyphenated.

The son of a public prosecutor who worked in Bulawayo, he moved to Scotland when aged 17 to study law at Edinburgh University and later taught the subject at Queen's University, Belfast.

Returning to Africa in 1981 and teaching law at Botswana University in addition to co-authoring in 1992 *The Criminal Law of Botswana*, he later returned to Scotland where he became Professor of Medical Law at Edinburgh University.

Now a full-time author but also Emeritus Professor of Law at the university, his works include the *No. 1 Ladies Detective Agency* series, *The Sunday Philosophy Club* series and the *44 Scotland Street* series, while in 2006 he was appointed a CBE for services to literature.

With posts that have included chairman of the ethics committee of the British Medical Journal and vice-chairman of the Human Genetics Commission of the United Kingdom, he is also a committed conservationist.

In 2014 he purchased the Scottish Hebridean chain of uninhabited islands the Cairns of Coll, and stated:

"I intend to do absolutely nothing with them, and to ensure that, after I am gone, they are held in trust, unspoilt and uninhabited, for the nation.

"I want them kept in perpetuity as a sanctuary for wildlife – for birds and seals and all the other creatures to which they are home."

On screen, **Phil McCall** was the Scottish actor of television and film born in Glasgow in 1925.

Film credits include the 1969 *Ring of Bright Water* and the 1996 *Breaking the Waves*, while television credits include *Dr Finlay's Casebook*, *Monarch of the Glen* and *Coronation Street*; chairman for a number of years of the Scottish committee of the actors' union Equity, he died in 2002.

On the television screen in contemporary times, **Davina McCall** is the presenter and former model born in 1967 in Wimbledon, London; presenter from 2000 to 2010 of the reality show *Big Brother*, other shows she has hosted include *The Million Dollar Drop*, *The Jump* and *Lost Family*.

Bearers of the McCall name and its popular spelling variant 'MacColl' have also excelled in the highly creative world of art.

Born in Glasgow in 1859, **Dugald Sutherland MacColl** was the Scottish watercolour painter, influential art critic and author who served as keeper of the Tate Gallery, London from 1906 to 1911.

A critic for publications including the *Spectator* and the *Saturday Review* and awarded the 1945 James Tait Black Memorial Prize for his biography *Philip Wilson Steer*, he died in 1948.

In a much different artistic genre and milieu, **Robert McCall** was the American conceptual artist famed for his works of 'space art.'

Born in 1919 in Columbus, Ohio and having worked as an illustrator for *Life* magazine, he created artwork for films including *2001: A Space Odyssey* and *Star Trek: The Next Generation*.

He died in 2010, while his work is found on U.S. postage stamps and stunning murals in the National Air and Space Museum, Washington, D.C., and the Lyndon B. Johnson Space Center in Houston, Texas.